Thriving On Who You Are

SAMSON UMURHURHU

THRIVING ON WHO YOU ARE

ISBN: 978-978-792-025-1

Published by:
Zayzee Limited
South Pointe Estate, Off Orchid Hotel Road, Lekki, Lagos, Nigeria.
+234 8120259068
zayzeeblog@gmail.com
www.zayzeewrites.com

Dedication

To all who want to thrive on their uniqueness

Table of Contents

Acknowledgements

I felt like a conduit which the ideas for this book freely flowed through, and in just three weeks, the manuscript was ready. For this, I am grateful for the calling and special favour on my life.

I'll like to specially thank Carol, my dear wife, who deployed her uniqueness to be complementary to who I am and was there to support and provide encouragement throughout this work. I also thank our two special children, Aghogho and Ejiro, for their input.

Uzezi Adesite, my editor and publisher, I thank her for her immense understanding and guidance to get this book out in record time

Preface

Every human possess immense value that mankind needs. We are made for lifelong relevance in contributing this value to different aspects of our world. We have been designed to reach beyond ourselves to positively impact others.

We are indeed all different, and there isn't a particular way for all to live life. There's also no specific approach to the issues that show up every day. We approach life differently and have individual ways that best suit us to thrive. I can thrive. You can thrive.

Your power, as well as your advantage, is that you are you. This is your leverage for contributions and to making a difference.

For you to thrive, how best you know who you are, and your ability to deploy and apply the knowledge of who you are, capitalising on your uniqueness, could be the factor that sets you apart and gives you an edge.

When everyone can do the same thing the same way, it becomes commonplace. When you can do it your own way, with elevated value added to others, you position yourself to be sought after by your particular target audience or market.

It is important that you know you and the worth of who you are. Understand that you're an embodiment of solutions that others need. Your background, experiences, education, skills and others make you special. You are a peculiar brand. You are a treasure. You count. You matter. You are a part of someone else's survival kit and enablement to thrive. Be intentional about who you are and thrive when and where others are holding back.

With prevailing circumstances in life, many people are losing the true sense of who they are. This leads to a loss of personal value, and in some cases to even a sense of worthlessness despite the fact they could be 'diamonds in the rough'.

At any point in our lives, we have a choice to reassess our knowledge of who we are, and the worth or value that is packaged within us. When we recognise that within us is the capacity to thrive, we have opportunities to correct and adjust when we fall short, and as we deem necessary, so we can harness our inner treasure to make a difference for others.

There will always be odds or challenges in life. Thriving against these could be what marinates your life to become of exceptional worth to impact and build others, and provide the launch pad for others to follow their path with accelerated progress.

You don't have to remain where you currently are for the rest of your life.

You can thrive on who you are.

THRIVE

How do I view the term 'Thrive'?

Some other words that easily come to my mind, which reflect what I mean and want to say or describe are amongst others:

flourish, overcome, do well, blossom, prosper, rise, achieve success, shine, expand, develop, grow, stand out, turn out well, conquer, fly high … on the foundation of who you are.

Thrive on the foundation of who you are. Expand on it.

How Do You Thrive?

When you're ***thriving***, you're moving towards your goals and vision, in the midst of and despite your challenging situations and events. In the process, you keep adapting, adjusting, evolving and coming out better equipped to live life, leveraging on your newly acquired experiences and competencies in helping others become better.

At the moment, you may think or believe you are in the shadow of who you desire to be. But you are still you. You can tap into relevant resources to develop what it takes to become the real you, and for you to grow in the confidence of who you really are. You will have to evolve to align your thoughts, language and actions to continuously unleash you to the level of mastery and excellence.

Where You Are Is A Good Place To Start Thriving.

T.H.R.I.V.E

T - The situation which you may currently be in, which needs intervention

H - Happenings and effects, impacts or manifestations of the situation

R - Root cause(s) identification for resolution

I - Ideal state, or the imagined outcome or end state you desire, and the gap identified and established against current reality

V - Verification and validation of the options available to you for adoption to move towards your goal(s)

E - Execute and embed your option(s) with specific action steps to move you to your desired end state, and thrive while tracking your progress.

Yes. YOU CAN THRIVE. It will not be an overnight event. It will involve a process. We all have things to work on to become better and to enable us to thrive. When you follow the process and work on becoming better, you can be in the crowd and still be spotted and recognised for who you are.

Everyone starts from a different place and follows a different path. In this book, I have provided thoughts and effective strategies you can deploy to THRIVE on who you are. The essence is not for you to be reckless with who you are, but to be responsible and accountable to yourself and all in optimising the value of being you — be seen, recognised, respected, and rewarded for who you are.

One

You Are Unique; We Are Different And It's Okay

I was at a company's cocktail event to celebrate the accomplishment of a big and impactful company project. The project was critical for the organisation's business sustainability. It was delicate, complex and complicated, as well as expensive, and required different expertise and people specifically chosen from across the organisation.

The room was packed with a couple of executives. That event remains one amazing experience that illustrates how unique and different we are. It helped me realise how we can collectively contribute to producing amazing results. That realisation was very significant for me.

The common denominator for that event was that a rare achievement was made by people who were different. The people gathered in the event's hall were from different backgrounds, gender, generations, experiences, expertise, personalities, nationalities and much more. Each of the individuals made a unique contribution and everyone was delighted with the outcome. In respect of the fun factor, there was more than enough to eat and drink as we celebrated, with beautiful music in the background. Even the lighting combination was stunning. Everything was complementary to the mood of that evening.

Some of the executives were chatty and loud, in reminiscence of their being selected for the project and their unique contributions which boosted the potential of the company for the future. Other executives took their finger food and drinks quietly. Some clustered in relatively large groups of fives and more, others hung together in twos or threes. Yet others were just on their own. Everyone had a choice to enjoy the celebration the way they pleased.

Some of the conversations that evening reflected on prolonged working hours, time away from family, disagreements and quarrels that had to be resolved, tight timelines to deliver targets, mistakes to be rectified, fun, breakthrough moments, celebrations and more. It was a tough, rough and sweet experience.

Some of the executives stayed for a short time, as there was no official time scheduled for the cocktail to end. Some others took their time, enjoying their interactions, their meals and drinks. The whole atmosphere was animated, revealing the extraordinary beauty our uniqueness and differences can bring.

At the end of that event, the company's objective of celebrating unity in diversity amongst its functions and people was massively achieved. Each executive was recognised for whom they were on the project, their contributions highlighted, and they were respectively rewarded for their roles. It was a display and an affirmation of each executive thriving on whom they were.

As I left, I kept savouring the experience. I particularly kept reflecting on the power of the personal choices of the executives who worked on the project. How they showed up, self-presented, collaborated, persevered and contributed selflessly to the various demands. Each chose to ensure overall success. The failure of one was the failure of all.

Despite all the odds, the goal was achieved and while we gathered to celebrate success, something had happened during the process or experience that got us to that day — we were more equipped and prepared to face life and career issues to keep thriving.

As an analogy, I see what happened on the project, and at the event, as a semblance of the beauty and splendour we can experience when we celebrate and allow our uniqueness, diversity and differences to come to play in our lives and career.

Everyone can thrive on who they are and stand out in respect of the value they bring. There are needs all around us and each one of us is uniquely equipped to contribute to being the solution. A lot has to do with the choices we make, in knowing who we really are, identifying and growing our specific gifts and value contributions, and evolving into who we are made to be.

Oftentimes we get distracted and lose our individuality because we want to please others or become like them. There are things around us that shift our focus from thoroughly mining, processing and possessing who we are. These may include:

- Yourself
- Family
- Business/Job
- Society
- People/Friends
- Cravings/Things
- Others

You are unique in who you are and what you bring. Your differentiating factor is YOU. Take a look at the following questions and attempt to answer them:

- What are you made of, and what are you made for?
- What are your specific gifts?
- How developed are these gifts?
- In which area(s) can they be most effective in

being of help to others? Where are they most needed?

- What will it take for you to be the go-to resource in your field and team?
- Who will you serve? How will you serve them? When?
- What is holding you back, or standing in your way?

It is a fact that the achievements of an organisation are the results of the collective efforts of the individuals in that organisation. Each individual is talented in a different way and has the capacity to capitalise on his or her uniqueness and special value add that brings about what would have been impossible without the individual unique contributions.

Having the capacity to capitalise on our uniqueness and special value add comes through the power of our well-informed choices. Choose to thrive. Choose who you are and make the best out of it in any given situation. Choose to thrive in the little things and build to thrive in the big things. Choose what you know how to do to thrive—this is being intentional and being a representative of the true value of who you are.

Learn to see others from the perspective of who they are, and not from the point of view of bias, stereotype and judgment. See the difference different people can bring.

If you are ever going to thrive, you have to believe that you have what it takes. Choose well and grow up on a healthy diet of spotting and developing your specific gifts and strengths to contribute to the overall good. Do not make decisions that compromise the core values that enable you uniquely contribute to the betterment of the world. Those you are called to serve are waiting for you. Share who you are with your world. Seek the right help and support if you need one.

Two

Discovering & Finding Who You Really Are

It's your responsibility to know who you are and be the subject-matter expert in ways you impact and add value to situations and others. Oftentimes, some people expect others to do this for them.

Self-discovery is not a destination to arrive at. It is a continuous and ongoing process that's lifelong because self-knowledge unfolds progressively.

Having and developing a good insight into who you are can make your life more meaningful, especially in the direction and path you're meant to take. It has the potential for you to better understand yourself and others. It can provide you with practical resources for visioning and letting go of what does not serve you. It may take time and effort, but it's a worthwhile exercise. It can be the difference that gives you an edge and makes you stand out. When you base your decisions, as well as respond to changes, challenges and opportunities of life on who you are, your potential to thrive is also amplified.

The process of self-discovery could be different

for everyone. For some people, it may extend to discovering purpose. Here are a few ideas on how to discover who you are:

1. Self Leadership

Be self-led to want to know you. Often, pause to look at who you are. Take responsibility. Become curious. Deliberately explore and grow your self-knowledge by answering relevant questions:

a. What do you know already about who you are, and what you were made and equipped to do?
b. What impacts did you have in your childhood?
c. What excellent work have you done in the past?
d. What do you naturally pay attention to?
e. Which activities do you do and enjoy with high energy levels?
f. What do you perceive as your natural bent (your disposition or inclination)? What do you lean towards?
g. What are you created for?

h. What are your thoughts on your purpose and calling?
i. To whom are you called?

Your responses to the above amongst others could provide some insights into who you are.

Be aware of the world around you and how you respond to it. Discover yourself through observations and experience. Have the courage to be different and consider the path that most naturally optimises what unfolds for you.

2. Consistent Valuable Feedback

Learn what others perceive about you:

a. How do you self-present and come across?
b. What impacts do you make?
c. Who are your significant others and confidants, and what will you consider to be some of their genuine impressions of you?
d. Who are those you know that have genuine testimonies of how they discovered themselves

and well evolved? How can possible feedback and insights from them help you?

e. What is consistent across the feedback you receive?
f. What are the different pieces of evidence that support the views?
g. How open are you to assessing what you hear?
h. What are you sensing?
i. How does the emerging information resonate with you?
j. What steps are necessary for adaptation?

3. Undertake Relevant Psychological/Personality Tests

Psychological/Personality tools/instruments are supposed to produce non-judgmental outcomes that help in understanding the fundamental style and patterns that shape individual behaviour.

Search for tools which have high validity outcomes and results. Some of such tools are Gallup's Strengths-Finder, Myers-Briggs, DISC, and others. Go further and ask for relevant professional support and guidance as there are many in the market. Get certified professionals and coaches to debrief you and/or coach you through your report to optimise benefits. Possible questions you may be asked for feedback on your report and which could facilitate further discussion with you may include the following amongst others:

a. What was your first reaction to the report on you?
b. What has the report helped you to discover about yourself?
c. Which parts surprised you?
d. What comments confirm what you believe to be true?
e. What are you pleased about?
f. What concerns you?
g. What patterns do you see emerging?
h. What issues or comments do you wish to further clarify?
i. Others

The conclusions could serve as inputs into your

personal development planning process as you think about what you have learnt about yourself, and the changes you wish to make.

4. Conceptualise Who You Are And Want To Be From The Different Input Sources

a. What do you see emerging?
b. What is the overall picture that you sense as your originality?
c. Do you have a clear understanding of your passion that conveys your authentic image?
d. What are you made of, and made for?
e. What makes you unique and special?
f. How will you focus on investing and developing who you are, to the level of mastery and excellence?
g. How will you use the information and data gathered from item No. 3 above of this Chapter, together with your other discoveries, to stand out from the crowd?
h. What do you perceive as your value? How

transformational is it, to you, and as your asset to use in your work with others?

i. How intimately connected, and at peace, are you with the concept of you that is coming up for you?
j. How has this exercise helped you see yourself for who you really are?
k. Which aspects of you do you need to develop to help take you to your next level?
l. What next steps are you willing and ready to consider?

The above and more can be useful approaches toward discovering who you are. You're in charge of your journey of self-discovery and how you capitalise on your uniqueness and optimise the benefits.

Be honest with yourself and build your life on who you are. Do not be moved by what and who you are not but by what you have, and who you are. Be in the category of those who desire to know who they really are, visualise who they could become, and are willing to do the work to become that someone. It takes some work and courage to be exceptional. Since you cannot run away from who you are, the best policy is to know you, stay with you, live you, deliver your value, and enjoy you.

Make every day count by contributing value from who you are and making a positive impact and difference for others. Beautify the world by being you. Leverage your personal twist, style and theatre, and learn to show your best every day, taking you to better and bigger heights.

Pull everything that you have become an embodiment of into convergence role(s). How this comes together will truly represent the worth of what you bring, and will be your greatest unique advantage for success and thriving.

Allow your acquired knowledge of who you are to enable you to do what you have not done before, to get to your next level. Our relationship with others, oftentimes, is a reflection of our relationship with ourselves. Your newly acquired knowledge of who you are will also enable you to see others differently, for who they are.

Now that you are more aware of who you are, aim to become more skilful in positioning you as a strategic advantage. Own who you are and find a style that you can call your own — a style that works in your situations and for you to deliver your best, and live who you are with confidence.

We lead from the position of who we are - who we are shows in our leadership. Take relevant risks and seize opportunities to evolve and add value.

Deploy you by coming up with a personal game plan to connect who you are to the fulfilment of your dreams and visions, for your success, to thrive and to update your plan(s) as you evolve.

Be accountable, even if you have to do things differently. Learn to serve every day wherever you find the need you can meet. Impact those you are called to, and in the process create your unique brand. This is how to find purpose and it will give you a reason for living.

When you master who you are, and adequately apply yourself, you will become a masterpiece.

Three

Life Formative School — My Personal Case Study & Lessons On Thriving

Over time, my background of fears, doubts, anxieties and uncertainties, was transformed into a life and career of great value-add, and impact on others. Yours can as well.

My dad had five wives and 33 biological children. We all lived together in the same compound in my village. I saw as a child, how my dad coped with his enormous responsibilities.

Our parents loved us and did their best for every one of us. However, in our context, I anchored my thinking early, that there weren't many visible established systems that could support me to succeed and thrive.

It was a feat for my dad to fund my education up to obtaining a Bachelor's degree. This qualified me for the compulsory one-year National Youths' Service Corps (NYSC) assignment. Done with my NYSC, I met my dad and told him I had gained admission to study for my Master's degree programme.

My dad looked at me and said, "Son, I am very proud

of you. But you know I also have to give other children the opportunity to be as well educated as you have become. You know how many of your siblings are in school right now, and the others also have to be educated. I cannot add your Master's degree expense responsibilities to what I have on hand."

I understood exactly what my dad meant. I wasn't inconsiderate to think or expect him to add another expense to his huge responsibilities. I had planned ahead of time and embraced a frugal lifestyle that helped me save enough to pay for my Master's degree programme from my monthly National Youth's Service allowances. My dad was surprised and relieved when I told him this.

My background situation taught me early to take personal responsibility. My mind was made up not to be held hostage and pigeonholed by my family's circumstances. I believed I had the opportunity for a new chance, and to create and walk my path. I saw the possibility of a different kind of life for me and I pursued it.

The future does not just happen. It takes intentionality to invest in creating the future of your desire. What you go through in life are seeds that have ways of shaping and equipping you. My background played a vital role in making me unique and special. I also exercised my power to choose in respect of what kind of influence my past could permanently have on me. I have become qualified by what I have gone through, and what I've allowed to be deposited in me. This has become my authority and license for who I am. I often remind myself that everybody is not like me. Not everyone can see and handle things the way I do.

Some people see what I have been able to achieve in life and my career as a mystery. I came from 'nowhere', worked in a government establishment, and got a widely advertised job in a critical role with Nestle in Nigeria (a big multinational company) where I knew nobody. When I resumed, I was told I was the solution to the problem they wanted to solve.

After six years with Nestle in Nigeria, I rose to the position of Head of Human Resources and became a member of the Executive Management Committee of the Company. Two years later, I became the Head of Human Resources for Nestle, Central & West Africa, covering 23 countries. This position started my journey as an expatriate outside my country, into the Nestle world.

Three years into my role in Central & West Africa, I was moved to the Nestle Group Headquarters in Switzerland, with an appointment letter and a briefing that I will be at the Head Office for 2-3 years. I ended up in various roles at the Nestle Headquarters Office in Switzerland for 12 years. Wow!

Many of those years abroad on expatriation, my family and I had to live managing uncertainties. I wasn't sure when the company would call me and announce my next role and location. In my more than 20 years of working with the Nestle Group, I was posted to 5 countries, held 7 job roles, and travelled to many parts of the world.

My experience helped me understand that growth is a process. Progress is a process. At every stage, I learnt to leverage my uniqueness, strengths, competencies/ capabilities and character to give and deliver my best. In some cases, I added massive value above what was expected from me.

In the course of my career, I met with, and in some cases, worked with some of the best professionals in different fields. This in itself presented challenges and opportunities. I also met and worked with people who could not deliver on the expectations of their roles, and had to be managed in line with due process. In everything, I had to factor in building my competencies and using my contexts to step more into whom I could be.

I heavily invested in self-education and self-taught in many other areas. I got feedback and adjusted. I learnt that winning and not winning was part of life. I took steps even when I was scared and in doubt. There were times I even felt not ready and well prepared for my next move. But as I moved, I discovered I was going through transformational processes that made me realise that any role I held, was the bridge and connection to the next.

I spent a lot of time out of our home on business trips. I spent sleepless nights reflecting and strategising on handling certain crises. I was involved in several delicate, tough and difficult conversations. There were pressures and battles on the functional front from colleagues, peers as well as at corporate levels. Nevertheless, there were also a lot of joy, fun and celebrations. All these provided opportunities for growth into my uniqueness and greatness in ways I never imagined and expected.

I have made a bit of investment in developing my self-awareness and this has helped me to deploy who I know I am. Wherever I have worked, I have given my all and my results represented me. Over time, I found shreds of evidence of my core traits, identified as patterns in my life and career.

Competencies are nearly always the product of several strengths in combination. The observed patterns were part of my vital tools and strategies for thriving in situations. They played major roles as underlying factors in my contributions and successes. They spoke for me. They were my advertisers and brand conveyors. Some of the unique attributes identified amongst others in my life and career included:

a. My love for channelling my mental, emotional and physical strengths into things that intrigue me.
b. Pinpointing subtle differences between people, and recognising people's unique styles, as well as helping them see how their special talents, knowledge and skills benefit others.
c. Employment of lots of humour and laughter as tools of work, and often calm.
d. My determination and interest in sharing knowledge and my skills with people who can

benefit and I welcome opportunities to spend time with them, while particularly enjoying the company of people who look forward to the future.

e. Pursuits of excellence and high-quality service delivery; responsive to the mood of the organisation.
f. Building on the power of collaboration, stirring people's enthusiasm with what I have been told is my cheerful exuberance for life and sharing my complete joy with others.
g. Quickly acting on what I am convinced about and my love for launching value-adding projects, instead of just talking about them, as I believe in results because they easily speak for themselves.
h. Promoting harmonious living within multi-racial, multi-national and multi- religious groups in line with organisations' principles and values.
i. Placing a lot of importance and focus on the

purpose and importance of what is before me, rather than just on the monetary rewards that accompany accomplishment and success.

j. My ideals and core values influencing how I spend my time and use my talents in contributing to creating better organisations.
k. Overcoming personal limiting beliefs and taking on meaningful new responsibilities and challenges, even if I'm not too sure I'm perfectly ready for it, and/or have all it takes for success. I learnt to take on things I have not done before and was willing to let things change as they should.

Additionally, I listened to my inner voice— the intuitive promptings within me—and relied on relevant guidance which resulted in my getting ahead, rather than just relying on my head knowledge. This has played several significant roles in my life and career. This is my way of tapping into my Christian faith and putting my Creator in the picture and in the midst of what I do.

I saw and still see myself as a vessel to positively impact those within my sphere of influence, and make a meaningful difference. My faith provided a foundational perspective for my existence.

I have thrived on who I am. My uniqueness has been the foundation of my approach to my work and my life. This made me embrace my career and become fulfilled. Being consistent in applying who I am to what I do has been very liberating and a source of joy to me. It has also led to different successes and it enables me to keep thriving.

I have worked in particularly demanding and tough business roles and operating environments, and found that being a good fit for your role, and being courageous to act outwardly on who you are, in alignment with your organisation's culture, values and principles amongst others, provides you with a solid foundation for thriving.

Pulling everything together—who I have become an embodiment of—into convergence roles in post-paid employment is now my new adventure. How this comes together will truly represent the worth I bring, and will be my greatest unique advantage for thriving in building my entrepreneurial work in a fast-changing and shifting world.

Four

Your Game Plan And Platform For Thriving

Getting to where you want to go can be made easier when you set your intentions and come up with a plan. When you have no plan (no matter how rough), a roadmap, or a strategy, going where you want to go and getting to your destination can be a challenge.

My desire has been to do something meaningful and fulfilling based on who I am after paid employment. I never wanted to be in the category of some career professionals, who become a shadow of who they were when their career in paid employment ends.

I feel privileged with my varied, challenging and rich career experiences and exposures. Coupled with my make-up and uniqueness, including my family, I knew I could position myself for lifelong relevance in adding value and making a difference for people.

For a game plan—to inspire you to create yours—I will illustrate, using my **Five Pillar Roadmap Framework**. This framework has helped me stay on course in the process of conceiving and executing dreams and visions to the finish line. My illustration will show how I am applying the framework to the vision I was inspired to birth for my post-paid employment signature role, the steps taken, and the best way in delivering the role, given my specific circumstances (that is, for me and my family).

1. Crafting a Vision That Improved My View of the Short-term

Crafting a long-term vision for my life and career enabled me to put the short term into proper perspective. This made it easier for me to know what to either embrace or eliminate in my daily choices. Every moment came as an opportunity to re-evaluate the options before me, and the decision to be made.

More than 10 years ahead of time, I envisioned a good life in self-work and entrepreneurship after paid employment. This did not imply that I had to abandon my present for the future. Rather, I knew I had to do well in my job and career to secure a fruitful tomorrow. I understood that my good results in the present would be the red carpets that would lead to my tomorrow. In the future, I saw myself and my family owning and running an enterprise with different platforms for empowering people in various areas of life and career.

This vision was a convergence role—quite a unique combination—that brought together the key ingredients that made me who I believed I am. I saw a one-stop hospitality facility where we hosted clients, including venues for social events, workshops and persons on short vacations. I saw my speaking, coaching, writing, consulting, leadership development, hospitality and other skill sets, all coming to play in impacting and empowering people. I saw relevant family members at work, as well as a team of talented individuals who had bought into the vision, coming in at various stages to support the work. This was a sweet spot for me, and definitely my signature role, which I have embodied, got what it takes to deliver, with fun and to thrive.

The concept was huge and expensive. I shared the vision with my family. We discussed and agreed. We adopted the draft vision storyboard I presented, and pasted it on the wall in a strategic part of our home. This became a visual image we saw every day, and became a vital input document guiding our savings, spending, investments and other key decisions, on a day-to-day basis.

2. Implementing Small Changes for 'Critical Marginal Gains' In Realising My Overall Goal

My family and I believed in the crafted vision. We were motivated, knowing that growth involves taking many small steps—which we did over the years—not just a few giant leaps. Improvement is a journey (a process), and not a destination (not an event). The journey of improvement does not end. We stayed dedicated to practising and improving our game plan every day with discipline, focus and consistency.

I worked with a professional coach and shared my learnings with my family. This helped us break the big post-paid employment vision down into different project phases and bite-size assignments with timelines. The bite-size assignments included putting up brick and mortar buildings, purchase of relevant equipment, I and relevant family members progressively acquiring new competencies in the areas we identified gaps amongst others.

We focused, one day at a time, on what was in front of us. These provided the stepping stones and a bridge to what was ahead. We found this process to be the most viable and sustainable strategy for our future while I was still in paid employment.

3. **Taking Personal Ownership to Excel in My Life, and Calling**

In the areas within our capability, we took our future into our hands. We knew that if we were not intentionally involved, the dream will remain a dream. I and my family self-sponsored and made massive investments in knowledge and ideas. We made time for what had to be done and ensured funds were available. We invested emotions, sought consultations and deferred certain momentary pleasures amongst others while ensuring we enjoyed and lived the best life for the moment, as we kept executing the plan for the future.

4. **Remaining Focused and Determined in the Face of Obstacles, Even When Results Were Slow in Coming**

While executing the vision, my family and I were out of my country on expatriation. Some of the plans being implemented—such as the physical building project—were going on back in my country. We received progress updates from the developer mainly through pictures that were mailed to us.

When we occasionally visited to see what was actually on the ground, what we saw were not actually as we were made to believe. There were issues with the quality of materials used. We lost time on meeting deadlines among other challenges. We fought doubts as we deliberated whether or not to continue with the project. We had to take tough decisions, including a decision about changing the existing developer. The new developer we appointed condemned and wrote off parts of the work that was already done by the previous developer, which resulted in us spending huge sums of money again for the rework.

In all, we resolved and decided to always figure out how to overcome obstacles on our paths, and stay the course to finish well and strong. We believed we found our future place with the vision. It was also clear to us, the specific audience we will target.

5. My Growth and Purpose-Driven Mindset Dominated My Agenda

We were poised to reach the destination we had set. It was top of mind that our project was a calling, and also rooted in our strengths and a combination of our unique attributes. We knew that when all is done, we will be enabled to impact and make great differences for many people.

We self-invested heavily in populating our Agendas and Calendars with activities that we trusted will deliver the future we hoped for. Plans do not execute themselves. We believed what we schedule, is what gets done. Keeping the appointments we set for ourselves in respect of what needs to be done in line with timelines was a priority. We had to commit ourselves, to actually doing what had to be done. We saw this as an inevitable part of the process for success.

Mission Accomplished

My consistent investment in myself and my identified core competencies for many years set me up for success on many important fronts and stages. Coupled with the execution of the roadmap and plan to work this out, after more than 10 years of coordinated efforts, discipline and focus, the overall blueprint has been satisfactorily accomplished. This also provided the confidence and the platform for me to leave paid employment and currently, my wife and myself have seamlessly transitioned into self-work and entrepreneurship.

The impact of your life is how much of a solution you are and the value you contribute. What will your own personal roadmap/plan look like? What effective system will work for you? Connect who you are to your plan for the fulfilment of your dreams and visions, and for you to keep thriving. Ask for relevant support where necessary.

Take a page from my **Five Pillar Roadmap Framework** and create yours today to let who you are, be in alignment with what you do. The information you do not implement cannot help you.

Five

You Can Become A Master

There is a point where you too can be a master. What you are and where you are at the moment matters. What you are working to become is also of great importance. Thriving helps you attain mastery of what you do. You evolve to become excellent.

I am not using the word 'master' in terms of gender, age or being superior. It is also not a concept of being perfect or being a guru. Rather, it is about having gone through an uncomfortable process that develops you to have an authentic voice in supporting and showing others possible lessons.

Life's school and experience have formed and equipped you. Your thriving is now about being a help to others who are facing the same frustrations and related challenges you faced when you were at that phase of life and career, and providing what you would have needed when you were going through your own 'bitter' experiences.

Some of the people who want to benefit from you want to get into your head and pick your brain. This will facilitate their thriving and coming out with a 'sweet' story such as yours. What you have gone through has become your license and authority, qualifying you to become a helper.

You have now come to know your mission, which may be channelled through a paid service or product or not. You see the possibilities in people. You are launching out intentionally, taking opportunities to help others with integrity, and for them to overcome the odds against them, so they can be transformed to thrive in a way that is a fit for who they are. Your story is not just an inspiration to others, it is also an inspiration for your life and work.

There is a common saying, that people who have been transformed, transform others. It is not the discomfort and challenges of life and career that transform people and make them strong. It is how we respond to the discomfort and challenges that make us come out better than we went in.

Your effective responses to your battles in secret and in

public, which you have overcome, make you invaluable. You may have been in that 'messy situation', but you are now 'cleaned up'. You have learnt and mined some insights, and have figured out your path that led to your freedom, and which possesses great value and worth to others.

Through your experience, you are now taking responsibility for having been equipped, to contribute to resolving the 'mess', or 'messes' of others. You have developed yourself, and your work, to be the go-to resource in your specific area or field. You elevated your work for service to other people. You are meeting needs; one person, or groups of persons at a time. You are helping them find their own path.

You have leveraged and capitalised on your uniqueness in overcoming your specific odd(s), in areas where many others still stall today. You have processed and packaged your valuable lessons, wisdom and expertise for others to possibly adapt in enhancing their progress.

Your experience and new competencies have put you a

couple of steps ahead of others. Those who believe and recognise that you can help bring out the best in them, stay connected to you. You see the vision and heartbeat of these needy people, and you want to, within your capacity and capability, help move them faster forward in a genuine way, on their path.

You generally present yourself, not just as a great marketer, but with sincere motives to serve people, let people know, and work with them to believe that they too can do it, and have their breakthroughs. You are poised to equip people to contribute their maximum to our world, based on who they are. You are a difference maker.

You support others in recognising blind spots. Based on trust and in the safety of relationships with you, you work with the people on how they can get past the blind spots. You are bold and intentional to facilitate breaking barriers on the way to their developing and thriving.

Ordinarily, people with these traits should be

commonplace. However, there is so much deception and flakiness. Given the big void and scarcity to find such people in our present day, I have decided to put this spotlight as an integral part of what makes people thrive on who they are, and become 'masters'.

Our world desperately needs genuine and authentic 'masters' in every facet to serve as guiding light, and provide workable paths and support to make a real difference for others.

I have come in contact with some of such people I regard as masters. I met some in person, others through their work like books, videos and other materials. They left transformational impacts and deposits on my life that gave me valuable perspectives for growth and enhanced my capacity to thrive on who I am.

It is not too late for anyone to desire to become a master. It is also never too late to seek a master.

Your being a master may not necessarily be related to your education or your level of academic qualifications—this does not make much difference in the lives of some people. Your being a master is based more on what life generally has built into you. Pressures make diamonds. In a unique way, you have become an embodiment of the treasures life has deposited in you. Those you serve can count on the practical, tangible and valuable results you bring.

The How To:

There is an endless list of how masters showcase their work and make the value they contribute known. A few examples might include the following:

a. Establish unique expertise in an area
b. Provide content/publication
c. Come up with projections, trends
d. Share personal testimonials — their journey with examples of handling situations
e. Provide pieces of evidence of practical results
f. Write books as a thought leader, a pacesetter

g. Be a movement leader for a cause your audience stands for
h. Support on a one-on-one basis, or in groups
i. Others

Meditate On This:

Where specifically have you identified as the area you have been equipped to make the greatest difference in becoming a master? Where you are currently, may just be the springboard in your evolution. You can become a master.

About The Author

Samson Umurhurhu is the CEO of Thrive Coaching Centre and HR Consulting Services Limited, a company that focuses on Leadership/ Executive, Talents/Strengths, Team/Group Coaching, as well as installing a Coaching Culture in Organisations.

He is also the Chief Business Facilitator of **The Thrive Place Limited,** a one-stop hospitality facility in Lagos, Nigeria.

Samson works with people to facilitate a smooth transition from paid employment to self-work and entrepreneurship.

He consults on Human Resources Strategies, especially in the areas of leadership development, employee engagement, and mobilization to realise set goals.

He holds a bachelor's degree in Sociology as well as a

master's degree in Industrial and Labour Relations. He is a Certified Professional Coach and a Certified Master Coach with the Center for Coaching Certification, USA. He is certified as a Strengths Coach by the Gallup Organization and credentialed by the International Coaching Federation as a Professional Certified Coach (PCC).

Samson has extensive work experience in various core areas of the Human Resources Function from the Country, Regional, and Zonal levels, up to the Group Head Office of the Nestle Group, and effectively supported top-level management committees.

He is passionate about partnering with his clients in a way that frees them up to thrive against their odds, drives results to boost their levels of success and achieves desired objectives.

Samson lives in Lagos, Nigeria with his family. ***Thriving On Who You Are*** is his third published book after ***Thriving Against The Odds – 15 Ideas For Professionals, Executives & Leaders To Sustain***

Advancement (2018), and ***Who Wants A Coach*** (2020).

www.thrivecoachandhr.com

Phone numbers: +234(0) 7081369471;

+234(0) 9063608987

E-Mail: info@thrivecoachandhr.com

www.ingramcontent.com/pod-product-compliance
Lightning Source LLC
La Vergne TN
LVHW050341160826
845677LV00014B/3729

* 9 7 8 9 7 8 7 9 2 0 2 5 1 *